INSTABILITY IN THE HINDU SHASTRAS: RUPTURES IN THE TEXTUAL INTEGRITY WITHIN THE MANUSCRIPTS.

Open Windows: A Feminist Research Center.

Published by

LIES AND BIG FEET

ISBN: 9384281182
ISBN-13: 978-9384281182

DEDICATION

To the Constitution of India.

CONTENTS

What we consider as infallible, sacred religious texts which comprise of "revealed knowledge" in the Hindu shastras is actually a compilation of many texts and changes must have occurred in them through centuries, as they were handed down through generations.

INTRODUCTORY COMMENTS.

It would be myopic if we refused to acknowledge that Max Mueller's (German philologist and Orientalist: 1823-1900) contribution to how the Hindu shastras were translated is essential to a nuanced understanding of how exactly were the editorial and textual processes involved in creating these texts. We can choose to disregard those parts of Muller's works that are a result of his personal biases which are symptomatic of Orientalist scholarship of the colonial period of the last two hundred years, but we cannot choose to undermine Mueller's mastery of Sanskrit. The following extract is from The *Complete Works of Swami Vivekananda* where Swami-ji himself compares Max Mueller's efforts as being akin to Sayana's commentaries.[1] We are therefore – coerced to also accept Max Mueller's translations of the Hindu shastras and self-reflexive commentaries on how he collated the different manuscripts of the Hindu shastras that were available to him.

---

[1] *The Complete Works of Swami Vivekananda*; available online.

(From the Diary of a Disciple)

(The disciple is Sharatchandra Chakravarty, who
published his records in a Bengali book, *Swami-Shishya-
Samvâda*, in two parts. The present series of
"Conversations and Dialogues" is a revised translation
from this book. Five dialogues of this series have already
appeared in the *Complete Works*,Volume 5)

[Place: Calcutta. year: 1897.]

For the last ten days, the disciple had been studying
Sâyana's commentary on the Rig-Veda with Swamiji,
who was staying then at the house of the late Babu
Balaram Bose at Baghbazar. Max Müller's volumes on
the Rig-Veda had been brought from a wealthy friend's
private library. Swamiji was correcting the disciple every
now and then and giving him the true pronunciation or
construction as necessary. Sometimes while explaining
the arguments of Sayana to establish the eternity of the
Vedas, Swamiji was praising very highly the
commentator's wonderful ingenuity; sometimes again
while arguing out the deeper significance of the doctrine,
he was putting forward a difference in view and
indulging in an innocent squib at Sayana.

While our study had proceeded thus for a while, Swamiji
raised the topic about Max Müller and continued thus:
Well, do you know, my impression is that it is Sayana

who is born again as Max Müller to revive his own commentary on the Vedas? I have had this notion for long. It became confirmed in my mind, it seems, after I had seen Max Müller. Even here in this country, you don't find a scholar so persevering, and so firmly grounded in the Vedas and the Vedanta. Over and above this, what a deep, unfathomable respect for Sari Ramakrishna! Do you know, he believes in his Divine Incarnation! And what great hospitality towards me when I was his guest! Seeing the old man and his lady, it seemed to me that they were living their home-life like another Vasishtha and Arundhati! At the time of parting with me, tears came into the eyes of the old man.

Disciple: But, sir, if Sayana himself became Max Müller, then why was he born as a Mlechchha instead of being born in the sacred land of India?

Swamiji: The feeling and the distinction that I am an Aryan and the other is a Mlechchha come from ignorance. But what are Varnâshrama and caste divisions to one who is the commentator of the Vedas, the shining embodiment of knowledge? To him they are wholly meaningless, and he can assume human birth wherever he likes for doing good to mankind. Specially, if he did not choose to be born in a land which excelled both in learning and wealth, where would he secure the large expenses for publishing such stupendous volumes? Didn't you hear that the East India Company paid nine lakhs of rupees in cash to have the Rig-Veda published? Even this money was not enough. Hundreds of Vedic Pundits had to be employed in this country on monthly stipends. Has anybody seen in this age, here in this country, such profound yearning for knowledge, such prodigious investment of money for the sake of light and learning? Max Müller himself has written it in his preface, that for twenty-five years he prepared only the manuscripts. Then the printing took another twenty years! It is not possible for an ordinary man to drudge for fortyfive years of his life with one publication. Just think of it! Is it an idle fancy of mine to say he is Sayana himself?

After this talk about Max Müller the leading of the Vedas was resumed.

1 THE UNSTABLE SACRED TEXT.

Manuscripts of the Hindu religious texts were often transferred onto print in the early years of print culture in colonial Bengal, India, (i.e. during the last decades of the eighteenth century) under the aegis of the East India Company sponsored Orientalists, but what exactly were the processes involved? How did native-brahmins look upon it as they assisted the Britishers in making the shift take place from a manuscript culture to a realm of print technology?

In 1825, Graves Chamney Haughton, a professor of Hindu Literature in the East India College, published an out-of-print text, William Jones's translation of the Sanskrit *Manava Dharma Shastra* or the *Institutes of Manu*.[2] Sir William Jones, an employee of the East India Company and referred to as the father of scientific linguistics and comparative philology, is a perfect example of a scholar

---

[2] Throughout, I will be referring to *Manusmriti* and *Manavadharma*, synonymously. I will be using the following text: *Manavadharmasastra, or, The Institutes of Manu*, according to the Gloss of Kulluka, comprising the Indian system of Duties, Religious and Civil. Verbally translated from the original, with a Preface by Sir William Jones, and Collated with the Sanskrit Text, by Graves Chanmey Haughton, Esq., Professor of Hindu Literature in the East India College. THIRD EDITION, edited by The Revd. P. Percival, Professor of Vernacular Literature, Presidency College, Madras. (Madras,J. Higginbotham: 1863).

who worked outside the Orientalist knowledge-making framework. He was also steeped in the culture of eighteenth century British print and had an immense trust in the veracity of printed texts. Haughton's prefatory note states that it was a new edition of Sir William Jones's translation; he writes that in his own text "the version of the learned translator has been carefully revised and compared" and that discrepancies would have been a result of the "variety of the manuscripts consulted by Sir William Jones." This observation provides us with historical documentation that there existed a "variety" of manuscripts that were consulted by these Orientalist scholars as they wrote their versions of the *Manusmriti*.

In 1794, the British government of India had Jones's *Manava Dharma* printed; Sir William Jones, writes in his preface about the processes involved in collaborating with the Brahmins in writing the text:

> ...[A]nd the brahman, who read it with me, requested most earnestly, that his name might be concealed; nor would he have read it for any consideration on a forbidden day of the moon,... so great, indeed, is the idea of sanctity annexed to this book, that, when the chief magistrate at Benaras endeavoured, at my request, to procure a Persian translation of it, before I had a hope of being at any time able to understand the original, the Pandits of his court unanimously and positively refused to assist in the work; nor should I have procured it at all, if a wealthy Hindu at Gaya had

not caused the version to be made by some of his dependants."

The question to ask is thus: did natives operate within a different parallel epistemic world where multiple manuscripts of the same text were seen as legitimate; moreover, why were the brahmins not necessarily keen to see their names on print, but neither were they hesitant to transfer a manuscript culture onto print? These early decades of colonial print can throw more light on the nature of religious-manuscripts that existed in India, before the advent of print in India. More importantly and is of relevance, is that: when we read a text like *Manusmriti*, why exactly should we assume that there exists an intact, untouched, version of the text?

Till as recently as two hundred years ago, India was a manuscript culture meaning that the printed text did not exist. When the transition took place from a manuscript culture to a print one, it seems to have taken place easelessly, implying that the shift was made without much murmurs and complaints from at least the native, elite sections of society. The Britishers, on the other hand, at seeing the beautiful manuscripts in Indian languages, must have been reminded of their pre-print past and a lot of care was taken to ensure that these manuscripts were well kept. When Tipu Sultan lost the Mysore wars (1780-90s), his library was also taken and a concern was raised by the Company soldiers as to how the manuscripts were to be kept safe: "That part of the library of the late Tippoo Sultan, which was presented by the army to the Court of Directors, is lately arrived in Bengal; the Governor-General strongly recommends that the Oriental manuscripts composing this collection, should be deposited in the library of the College of Fort William, and it is his intention to retain the manuscripts accordingly, until he shall receive the orders of the Court upon the subject."[3] There was no rampant erasure of the Indian manuscript past, and in fact, the Company was keen to preserve this aspect of Indian culture.

The larger question, though, is: can we ever take it for a given that what we know, in a definitive manner, as being central to the Hindu *shastras* can be construed as being infallible? - for all we know – these texts might have been amended and changes made as they were handed down generations. In the preface to his version of *Manavadharma*,

---

[3] *The Annals of the College of Fort William, from the Period of its Foundation.*Arranged and Published by Thomas Roebuck, Calcutta, Printed by Philip Periera at the Hindoostanee Press, 1819. "Introduction" pp. xxv. The report mentions the importance of preserving old manuscripts: "The preservation and augmentation of the Collection of Eastern Manuscripts, afford the only means of arresting the progressive destruction of Oriental learning. Since the dismemberment of the Muslim, those works have been dispersed over India, and have been exposed to the injuries and hazards of time, accident and neglect. It is worthy of the ambition of this great Empire to employ every effort of its influence in preserving from destruction and decay, these valuable records of Oriental history, Science and Religion." p. 114.

Sir William Jones wrote about the textual variations that existed and how he collated different versions that were available in manuscript form to arrive at his final text:[4]

> At length appeared KULLU'KA BHATTA; who, after a painful course of study and the collation of numerous manuscripts, produced a work, of which it may, perhaps, be said very truly, that it is the shortest, yet the most luminous, the least ostentatious, yet the most learned, the deepest, yet the most agreeable, commentary ever composed on any author [namely, Manu] ancient or modern, European or Asiatic. The Pandits care so little for genuine chronology, that none of them can tell me the age of KULLU'KA, whom they always name with applause; but he informs us himself, that he was a *Brahmin* of the *Varéndra* tribe, whose family had been long settled in *Gaur* or Bengal, but that he had chosen his residence among the learned on the banks of the holy river at Ka'si. His text and interpretation I have almost implicitly followed, though I had myself collated many copies of MANU, and among them a manuscript of a very ancient date: …

We can arrive at the obvious conclusion that William Jones consulted many textual variations of the *Manusmriti*, and if so, the implication is that there was no single authoritative

---

[4] *Manusmriti.*

text. If these texts that constitute our Hindu *shastras* are unreliable with numerous variants existing simultaneously, then it stands to reason that there is no authentic version that we can refer to as being the original. Who is to tell as to which part comprised "revealed knowledge" and which sections were subsequent add-ons?

2 EDITORIAL INTERVENTION IN RECUPERATING A MANUSCRIPT TEXT.

The following is an extract which allows us to understand how numerous manuscripts were consulted before the editor arrived at a version of a printed text.

MANUTIKASANGRAHA BEING A SERIES OF COPIUS EXTRACTS FROM SIX UNPUBLISHED COMMENTARIES OF THE CODE OF MANU.

EDITED BY JULIUS JOLLY. CALCUTTA: PRINTED BY J.W. THOMAS AT THE BAPTIST MISSION PRESS. AND PUBLISHED BY THE ASIATIC SOCIETY. 57 PARK STREET. 1885.

Preface

At the time when the plan of the present work was laid before the Council of the Asiatic Society, during my stay in India in the year 1883, the *Manavarthamuktavali* of Kullukabhatta was the only one Sanskrit Commentary of Manu extant in print, and the large number of printed editions of his celebrated composition offered a strange contrast with the entire neglect of the less famous, but more valuable and original works of the various other Commentators of the Code of Manu. It has been shown elsewhere that Kullukabhatta was a mere plagiary, and has generally copied the glosses of his predecessors Govindaraja without acknowledgement, or rather trying to veil the true nature of his own composition by indulging every now and then in ferocious attacks on the very work to which he was indebted to such a large extent. Indeed, the recovery of Govindaraja's *Manutika* has put Kulluka entirely in the shade, and the publication of the *Manutika*, which appears to have been composed as early as the twelfth or thirteenth century, had therefore to be considered as a special desideratum, especially as Kulluka's epitome of it consisted in many instances of insufficient and garbled extracts.

....

After having succeeded in securing a sufficient number of reliable MSS of all these Commentaries, I had to make up my mind about the way in which they should be edited. Though a new edition of Kulluka's *Manvarthamuktavali* might be dispensed with, for the abovementioned reasons, the size of the six remaining Commentaries was far too large to admit of my entertaining the hope of finding a publisher for a complete edition of these works. Moreover, it appeared quite doubtful whether a judicious selection from the glosses of the Commentators would not be in itself preferable to a publication of them *in extenso*, as it would facilitate for the reader the laborious task of gathering the really useful portions from among the vast amount of rubbish contained in the Commentaries. The Commentators of Manu, like most of their brethren in India, are only too fond of making a display of their learning, and are constantly indulging in learned but superfluous discussions and endless quotations of every sort. By omitting all such extraneous matter, it would be possible to reduce the size of the work to reasonable dimensions, without falling into the error of publishing garbled or insufficient extracts. This scheme was graciously approved of by the Council of the Asiatic Society, and the first and second parts of the Selections appeared in the *Bibliothecca Indica*, in 1885 and 1886.

...

In spite of these ample materials, however, the attempt to work out a really satisfactory edition of Medhatithi's voluminous work might have proved a failure, as all the hitherto available copies differ considerably, and are hopelessly corrupt in the eighth, ninth and twelfth chapters. Such being the case, it might seem the best course to bring the present work to a close with the third chapter, as the new result to be gained from an improved edition of the more important parts of the Commentaries might not have been sufficient to cause it to appear worthy of a Sanskrit scholar or of the Bibliotheca Indica to go again over ground already trodden. ...

The selections contained in the three parts of the *Manutikasangraha* cover about one-fourth part of the *Manava Dharmasastra*.

3 EXTRACTS FROM NUMEROUS TRANSLATIONS OF THE HINDU SHASTRAS.

THE WORKS OF MAX MUELLER

Max Mueller's translations of the Rig Veda reveal a self-reflexive sense of the role of an editor; and in fact – he transfers onto the editor an authorial function. The focus of these extracts from Mueller's works is to draw attention on how he collated different manuscripts and subsequently arrived at a definitive text. As readers situated in the present – we need to be able to understand that what constitutes our Hindu shastras and are disseminated in the public realm by the religious institutions all across India and the world -have actually gone through numerous editorial processes in the last two hundred years or so.

VEDIC HYMNS

PART I
HYMNS TO THE MARUTS, RUDRA, VÂYU, AND VÂTA

Translated by

F. MAX MÜLLER

Clarendon: Oxford University Press

[1891]⁵

Introduction.

…And there is this additional difficulty that when we deal

with inscriptions, we have at all events the text as it was

---

⁵ *Rig Veda Sanhita. The Sacred Hymns of the Brahmans*. Translated and
Explained by F. Max Mueller. London: Trubner and Co.(60 Paternoster Row,
1869.)

engraved from the first, and we are safe against later modifications and interpolations, while in the case of the Veda, even though the text as presupposed by the Prâtiśâkhyas may be considered as authoritative for the fifth century B.C., how do we know what changes it may have undergone before that time? Nor can I help giving expression once more to misgivings I have so often expressed, whether the date of the Prâtiśâkhyas is really beyond the reach of doubt, and whether, if it is, there is no other way of escaping from the conclusion that the whole collection of the hymns of the Rig-veda, including even the Vâlakhilya hymns, existed at that early time. The more I study the hymns, the more I feel staggered at the conclusion at which all Sanskrit scholars seem to have arrived, touching their age. That many of them are old, older than anything else in Sanskrit, their grammar, if nothing else, proclaims in the clearest way. But that some of them are modern imitations is a conviction that forces itself even on the least sceptical minds. Here too we must guard against positivism, and suspend our judgment, and accept correction with a teachable spirit. No one would be more grateful for a way out of the maze of Vedic chronology than I should be, if a more modern date could be assigned to some of the Vedic hymns than the period of the rise of Buddhism. But how can we account for Buddhism without Vedic hymns? In the oldest Buddhist Suttas the hymns of three Vedas are constantly referred to, and warnings are uttered even against the fourth Veda, the Âthabbana. The Upanishads also, the latest productions of the Brâhmana period, must have been known to the founders of Buddhism. From all this there seems to be no escape, and yet I must confess that my conscience quivers in assigning such compositions as the Vâlakhilya hymns to a period preceding the rise of Buddhism in India.

PREFACE

TO THE FIRST EDITION.

WHEN some twenty years ago I decided on undertaking the first edition of the two texts and the commentary of the Rig-veda, I little expected that it would fall to my lot to publish also what may, without presumption, be called the first translation of the ancient sacred hymns of the Brahmans. Such is the charm of deciphering step by step the dark and helpless utterances of the early poets of India, and discovering from time to time behind words that for years seemed unintelligible, the simple though strange expressions of primitive thought and primitive faith, that it required no small amount of self-denial to decide in favour of devoting a life to the publishing of the materials rather than to the drawing of the results which those materials supply to the student of ancient language and ancient religion. Even five and twenty years ago, and without waiting for the publication of Sâyana's commentary, much might have been achieved in the interpretation of the hymns of the Rig-veda. With the MSS. then accessible in the principal libraries of Europe, a tolerably correct text of the Samhitâ might have been published, and these ancient relics of a primitive religion might have been at least partially deciphered and translated in the same way in which ancient inscriptions are deciphered and translated, viz. by a careful collection of all grammatical forms, and by a complete intercomparison of all passages in which the same words and the same phrases occur. When I resolved to devote my leisure to a critical edition of the text and commentary of the Rig-veda rather than to an independent study of that text, it was chiefly from a conviction that the traditional interpretation of the Rig-veda, as embodied in the commentary of Sâyana and other works of a similar character, could not be neglected with impunity, and that sooner or later a complete edition of these works would be recognised as a necessity. It was better therefore to begin with the beginning, though it seemed hard sometimes to spend forty years in the wilderness instead of rushing straight into the promised land.

It is well known to those who have followed my literary publications that I never entertained any exaggerated opinion as to the value of the traditional interpretation of the Veda, handed down in the theological schools of India,

and preserved to us in the great commentary of Sâyana.
More than twenty years ago, when it required more courage
to speak out than now, I expressed my opinion on that
subject in no ambiguous language, and was blamed for it by
some of those who now speak of Sâyana as a mere drag in
the progress of Vedic scholarship. Even a drag, however, is
sometimes more conducive to the safe advancement of
learning than a whip; and those who recollect the history of
Vedic scholarship during the last five and twenty years,
know best that, with all its faults and weaknesses, Sâyana's
commentary was a sine quâ non for a scholarlike study of
the Rig-veda. I do not wonder that others who have more
recently entered on that study are inclined to speak
disparagingly of the scholastic interpretations of Sâyana.
They hardly know how much we all owe to his guidance in
effecting our first entrance into this fortress of Vedic
language and Vedic religion, and how much even they,
without being aware of it, are indebted to that Indian
Eustathius. I do not withdraw an opinion which I
expressed many years ago, and for which I was much
blamed at the time, that Sâyana in many cases teaches us
how the Veda ought not to be, rather than how it ought to
be understood. But for all that, who does not know how

much assistance may be derived from a first translation, even though it is imperfect, nay, how often the very mistakes of our predecessors help us in finding the right track? If now we can walk without Sâyana, we ought to bear in mind that five and twenty years ago we could not have made even our first steps, we could never, at least, have gained a firm footing without his leading strings. If therefore we can now see further than he could, let us not forget that we are standing on his shoulders.

I do not regret in the least the time which I have devoted to the somewhat tedious work of editing the commentary of Sâyana, and editing it according to the strictest rules of critical scholarship. The Veda, I feel convinced, will occupy scholars for centuries to come, and will take and maintain for ever its position as the most ancient of books in the library of mankind. Such a book, and the commentary of such a book, should be edited once for all; and unless some unexpected discovery is made of more ancient MSS., I do not anticipate that any future Bekker or Dindorf will find much to glean for a new edition of Sâyana, or that the text, as restored by me from a collation of the best MSS.

accessible in Europe, will ever be materially shaken.[6] It has taken a long time, I know; but those who find fault with me for the delay, should remember that few scholars, if any, have worked for others more than I have done in copying and editing Sanskrit texts, and that after all one cannot give up the whole of one's life to the collation of Oriental MSS. and the correction of proof-sheets. The two concluding

---

[6] Since the publication of the first volume of the Rig-veda, many new MSS. have come before me, partly copied for me, partly lent to me for a time by scholars in India, but every one of them belonged clearly to one of the three families which I have described in my introduction to the first volume of the Rig-veda. In the beginning of the first Ashtaka, and occasionally at the beginning of other Ashtakas, likewise in the commentary on hymns which were studied by native scholars with particular interest, various readings occur in some MSS., which seem at first to betoken an independent source, but which are in reality mere marginal notes, due to more or less learned students of these MSS. Thus after verse 3 of the introduction one MS. reads: sa prâha nripatim, râgan, sâyanâryo mamânugah, sarvam vetty esha vedânâm vyâkhyâtritvena, yugyatâm. The same MS., after verse 4, adds: ityukto mâdhavâryena vîrabukkamahîpatih, anvasât sâyamâkâryam vedârthasya prakâsane.

I had for a time some hope that MSS. written in Grantha or other South-Indian alphabets might have preserved an independent text of Sâyana, but from some specimens of a Grantha MS. collated for me by Mr. Eggeling, I do not think that even this hope is meant to be realised. The MS. in question contains a few independent various readings, such as are found in all MSS., and owe their origin clearly to the jottings of individual students. when at the end of verse 6, I found the independent reading, vyutpannas tâvatâ sarvâ riko vyâkhyâtum arhati, I expected that other various readings of the same character might follow.

volumes have long been ready for Press, and as soon as I can find leisure, they too shall be printed and published.

. . .

After these preliminary remarks I have to say a few words on the general plan of my translation.

I do not attempt as yet a translation of the whole of the Rig-veda, and I therefore considered myself at liberty to group the hymns according to the deities to which they are addressed. By this process, I believe, a great advantage is gained. We see at one glance all that has been said of a certain god, and we gain a more complete insight into his nature and character. Something of the same kind had been attempted by the original collectors of the ten books, for it can hardly be by accident that each of them begins with hymns addressed to Agni, and that these are followed by hymns addressed to Indra. The only exception to this rule is the eighth Mandala, for the ninth being devoted to one deity, to Soma, can hardly be accounted an exception. But if we take the Rig-veda as a whole, we find hymns, addressed to the same deities, not only scattered about in different books, but not even grouped together when they occur in one and the same book. Here, as we lose nothing by giving up the old arrangement, we are surely at liberty, for our own purposes, to put together such hymns as have a common object, and to place before the reader as much material as possible for an exhaustive study of each individual deity.

I give for each hymn the Sanskrit original[7] in what is known as the Pada text, i. e. the text in which all words (pada) stand by themselves, as they do in Greek or Latin, without being joined together according to the rules of Sandhi. The text in which the words are thus joined, as they are in all other Sanskrit texts, is called the Samhitâ text. Whether the Pada or the Samhitâ text be the more ancient, may seem difficult to settle. As far as I can judge, they seem to me, in their present form, the product of the same period of Vedic scholarship. The Prâtisâkhyas, it is true, start from the Pada text, take it, as it were, for granted, and devote their rules to the explanation of those changes

---

[7] A number of various readings which have been gleaned from Pandit Târânâtha's Tulâdânâdipaddhati (see Trübner's American and Oriental Literary Record, July 31, 1868) belong to the same class. They may be due either to the copyists of the MSS. which Pandit Târânâtha used while compiling his work, or they may by accident have crept into his own MS. Anyhow, not one of them is supported either by the best MSS. accessible in Europe, or by any passage in the Prâtisâkhya.

which that text undergoes in being changed into the Samhitâ text. But, on the other hand, the Pada text in some cases clearly presupposes the Samhitâ text. It leaves out passages which are repeated more than once, while the Samhitâ text always repeats these passages; it abstains from dividing the termination of the locative plural su, whenever in the Samhitâ text, i. e. according to the rules of Sandhi, it becomes shu; hence nadîshu, agishu, but ap-su; and it gives short vowels instead of the long ones of the Samhitâ, even in cases where the long vowels are justified by the rules of the Vedic language. It is certain, in fact, that neither the Pada nor the Samhitâ text, as we now possess them, represents the original text of the Veda. Both show clear traces of scholastic influences. But if we try to restore the original form of the Vedic hymns, we shall certainly arrive at some kind of Pada text rather than at a Samhitâ text; nay, even in their present form, the original metre and rhythm of the ancient hymns of the Rishis are far more perceptible when the words are divided, than when we join them together throughout according to the rules of Sandhi. Lastly, for practical purposes, the Pada text is far superior to the Samhitâ text in which the final and initial letters, that is, the most important letters of words, are constantly disguised, and liable therefore to different interpretations. Although in some passages we may differ from the interpretation adopted by the Pada text, and although certain Vedic words have, no doubt, been wrongly analysed and divided by Sâkalya, yet such cases are comparatively few, and where they occur, they are interesting as carrying us back to the earliest attempts of Vedic scholarship. In the vast majority of cases the divided text, with a few such rules as we have to observe in reading Latin, nay, even in reading Pâli verses, brings us certainly much nearer to the original utterance of the ancient Rishis than the amalgamated text.

The critical principles by which I have been guided in editing for the first time the text of the Rig-veda, require a few words of explanation, as they have lately been challenged on grounds which, I think, rest on a complete misapprehension of my previous statements on this subject.

As far as we are able to judge at present, we can hardly speak of various readings in the Vedic hymns, in the usual sense of that word. Various readings to be gathered from a collation of different MSS., now accessible to us, there are none. After collating a considerable number of MSS., I have succeeded, I believe, in fixing on three representative MSS., as described in the preface to the first volume of my edition of the Rig-veda. Even these MSS. are not free from blunders,—for what MS. is?—but these blunders have no claim to the title of various readings. They are lapsus calami, and no more; and, what is important, they have not become traditional.

The text, as deduced from the best MSS. of the Samhitâ text, can be controlled by four independent checks. The first is, of course, a collation of the best MSS. of the Samhitâ text. The second check to be applied to the Samhitâ text is a comparison with the Pada text, of which, again, I possessed at least one excellent MS., and several more modern copies. The third check was a comparison of this text with Sâyana's commentary, or rather with the text which is presupposed by that commentary. In the few cases where the Pada text seemed to differ from the Samhitâ text, a note was added to that effect, in the various readings of my edition; and the same was done, at least in all important cases, where Sâyana clearly followed a text at variance with our own.

The fourth check was a comparison of any doubtful passage with the numerous passages quoted in the Prâtisâkhya.

These were the principles by which I was guided in the critical restoration of the text of the Rig-veda, and I believe I may say that the text as printed by me is more correct than any MS. now accessible, more trustworthy than the text followed by Sâyana, and in all important points identically the same with that text which the authors of the Prâtisâkhya followed in their critical researches in the fifth or sixth century before our era.

…

Far be it from me to say that the editio princeps of the text thus constituted was printed without mistakes. But most of these mistakes are mistakes which no attentive reader could fail to detect. Cases like II, 35, 1, where gógishat instead of góshishat was printed three times, so as to perplex even

Professor Roth, or II, 12, 14, where sasamânám occurs three times instead of sasamânám, are, I believe, of rare occurrence. Nor do I think that, unless some quite unexpected discoveries are made, there ever will be a new critical edition, or, as we call it in Germany, a new recension of the hymns of the Rig-veda. If by collating new MSS., or by a careful study of the Prâtisâkhya, or by conjectural emendations, a more correct text could have been produced, we may be certain that a critical scholar like Professor Aufrecht would have given us such a text. But after carefully collating several MSS. of Professor Wilson's collection, and after enjoying the advantage of Professor Weber's assistance in collating the MSS. of the Royal Library at Berlin, and after a minute study of the Prâtisâkhya, he frankly states that in the text of the Rig-veda, transcribed in Roman letters, which he printed at Berlin, he followed my edition, and that he had to correct but a small number of misprints. For the two Mandalas which I had not yet published, I lent him the very MSS. on which my edition is founded; and there will be accordingly but few passages in these two concluding Mandalas, which

I have still to publish, where the text will materially differ from that of his Romanised transcript.

No one, I should think, who is at all acquainted with the rules of diplomatic criticism, would easily bring himself to touch a text resting on such authorities as the text of the Rig-veda. What would a Greek scholar give, if he could say of Homer that his text was in every word, in every syllable, in every vowel, in every accent, the same as the text used by Peisistratos in the sixth century B.C.! A text thus preserved in its integrity for so many centuries, must remain for ever the authoritative text of the Veda.

To remove, for instance, the eleven hymns 49-59 in the eighth Mandala from their proper place, or count them by themselves as Vâlakhilya hymns, seems to me, though no doubt perfectly harmless, little short of a critical sacrilege. Why Sâyana does not explain these hymns, I confess I do not know; but whatever the reason was, it was not because they did not exist at his time, or because he thought them spurious. They are regularly counted in Kâtyâyana's Sarvânukrama, though here the same accident has happened. One commentator, Shadgurusishya, the one most commonly used, does not explain them; but another commentator, Gagannâtha, does explain them, exactly as they occur in the Sarvânukrama, only leaving out hymn 58. That these hymns had something peculiar in the eyes of native scholars, is clear enough. They may for a time have formed a separate collection, they may have been considered of more modern origin. I shall go even further than those who remove these hymns from the place which they have occupied for more than two thousand years. I admit they disturb the regularity both of the Mandala and the Ashtaka divisions, and I have pointed out myself that they are not counted in the ancient Anukramanîs ascribed to Saunaka; (History of Ancient Sanskrit Literature, p. 220.) But, on the other hand, verses taken from these hymns occur in all the other Vedas; they are mentioned by name in the Brâhmanas (Ait. Br. V, 15; VI, 24), the Âranyakas (Ait. Âr. V, 10, p. 445), and the Sûtras (Âsv. Srauta Sûtras, VIII, 2, 3), while they are never included in the manuscripts of Parisishtas or Khilas or apocryphal hymns, nor mentioned by Kâtyâyana as mere Khilas in his Sarvânukrama.

…

. . .

It proves, unless all our views on the chronology of Vedic literature are wrong, that in the fifth century B.C. at least, or previously rather to the time when the Prâtisâkhya was composed, both the Pada and the Samhitâ texts were so firmly settled that it was impossible, for the sake of uniformity or regularity, to omit one single short a; and it proves à fortiori, that the hymn in which that irregular short a occurs, formed at that time part of the Vedic canon. I confess I feel sometimes frightened by the stringency of this argument, and I should like to see a possibility by which we could explain the addition, not of the Vâlakhilya hymns only, but of other much more modern sounding hymns, at a later time than the period of the Prâtisâkhyas. But until that possibility is shown, we must abide by our own conclusions; and then I ask, who is the critic who would dare to tamper with a canon of scripture of which every iota was settled before the time of Cyrus, and which we possess in exactly that form in which it is described to us by the authors of the Prâtisâkhyas? I say again, that I am not free from misgivings on the subject, and my critical conscience would be far better satisfied if we could ascribe the Prâtisâkhya and all it presupposes to a much later date. But until that is done, the fact remains that the two divergent texts, the Pada and Samhitâ, which we now possess, existed, as we now possess them, previous to the time of the Prâtisâkhya. They have not diverged nor varied since, and the vertex to which they point, starting from the distance of the two texts as measured by the Prâtisâkhya, carries us back far beyond the time of Saunaka, if we wish to determine the date of the first authorised collection of the hymns, both in their Pada and in their Samhitâ form.

...

If these arguments are sound, and if nothing can be said against the critical principles by which I have been guided in editing the text of the Rig-veda, if the fourfold check, described above, fulfils every requirement that could be made for restoring that text which was known to Sâyana, and which was known, probably 2000 years earlier, to the authors of the Prâtisâkhyas, what can be the motives, it may fairly be asked, of those who clamour for a new and more critical edition, and who imagine that the editio princeps of the Rig-veda will share the fate of most of the editiones principes of the Greek and Roman classics, and be supplanted by new editions founded on the collation of other MSS.?

...

It will be seen from these remarks that many things have to be considered before one can form an independent judgment as to the exact view adopted by Sâyana in places where he differs from other authorities, or as to the exact words in which he clothed his meaning. Such cases occur again and again. Thus in IX, 86, I find that Professor Aufrecht ascribes the first ten verses to the Akrishtas, whereas Sâyana calls them Âkrishtas. It is perfectly true that the best MSS. of the Anukramanikâ have Akrishta, it is equally true that the name of these Akrishtas is spelt with a short a in the Harivamsa, 11,533, but an editor of Sâyana's work is not to alter the occasional mistakes of that learned commentator, and Sâyana certainly called these poets Âkrishtas.

Verses 21-30 of the same hymn are ascribed by Professor
Aufrecht to the Prisniyah. Here, again, several MSS.
support that reading; and in Shadgurusishya's commentary,
the correction of prisniyah into prisnayah is made by a later
hand. But Sâyana clearly took prisnayah for a nominative
plural of prisni, and in this case he certainly was right. The
Dictionary of Böhtlingk and Roth quotes the Mahâbhârata,
VII, 8728, in support of the peculiar reading of prisniyah,
but the published text gives prisnayah. Professor Benfey, in
his list of poets (Ind. Stud. vol. iii, p. 223), gives prisniyoga
as one word, not prisniyogâ, as stated in the Dictionary of
Böhtlingk and Roth, but this is evidently meant for two
words, viz. prisnayo gâh. However, whether prisniyah or
prisnayah be the real name of these poets, an editor of
Sâyana is bound to give that reading of the name which
Sâyana believed to be the right one, i. e. prisnayah.

Again, in the same hymn, Professor Aufrecht ascribes
verses 31-40 to the Atris. We should then have to read
tritîye trayah. But Sâyana read tritîye trayah, and ascribes
verses 31-40 to the three companies together of the R*i*shis
mentioned before. On this point the MSS. admit of no
doubt, for we read: katurthasya ka dasarkasya âkrishtâ

mâshâ ityâdidvinâmânas trayo ganâ drashtârah. I do not say that the other explanation is wrong; I only say that, whether right or wrong, Sâyana certainly read trayah, not atrayah; and an editor of Sâyana has no more right to correct the text, supported by the best MSS., in the first and second, than in the third of these passages, all taken from one and the same hymn.

But though I insist so strongly on a strict observance of the rules of diplomatic criticism with regard to the text of the Rig-veda, nay, even of Sâyana, I insist equally strongly on the right of independent criticism, which ought to begin where diplomatic criticism ends. Considering the startling antiquity which we can claim for every letter and accent of our MSS., so far as they are authenticated by the Prâtisâkhya, to say nothing of the passages of many hymns which are quoted verbatim in the Brâhmanas, the Kalpa-sûtras, the Nirukta, the Brihaddevatâ, and the Anukramanîs, I should deem it reckless to alter one single letter or one single accent in an edition of the hymns of the Rig-veda. As the text has been handed down to us, so it should remain; and whatever alterations and corrections we, the critical Mlekkhas of the nineteenth century, have to propose, should be kept distinct from that time-hallowed inheritance. Unlikely as it may sound, it is true nevertheless that we, the scholars of the nineteenth century, are able to point out mistakes in the text of the Rig-veda which escaped the attention of the most learned among the native scholars of the sixth century B.C. No doubt, these scholars, even if they had perceived such mistakes, would hardly have ventured to correct the text of their sacred writings. The authors of the Prâtisâkhya had before their eyes or ears a text ready made, of which they registered every peculiarity, nay, in which they would note and preserve every single irregularity, even though it stood alone amidst hundreds of analogous cases. With us the case is different. Where we see a rule observed in 99 cases, we feel strongly tempted and sometimes justified in altering the 100th case in accordance with what we consider to be a general rule. Yet even then I feel convinced we ought not to do more than place our conjectural readings below the textus receptus of the Veda,—a text so ancient and venerable that no scholar of any historical tact or critical taste would venture to foist into it a conjectural reading, however plausible, nay, however undeniable.

...

The most powerful instrument that has hitherto been applied to the emendation of Vedic texts, is the metre. Metre means measure, and uniform measure, and hence its importance for critical purposes, as second only to that of grammar. If our knowledge of the metrical system of the Vedic poets rests on a sound basis, any deviations from the general rule are rightly objected to; and if by a slight alteration they can be removed, and the metre be restored, we naturally feel inclined to adopt such emendations. Two safeguards, however, are needed in this kind of conjectural criticism. We ought to be quite certain that the anomaly is impossible, and we ought to be able to explain to a certain extent how the deviation from the original correct text could have occurred. As this subject has of late years received considerable attention, and as emendations of the Vedic texts, supported by metrical arguments, have been carried on on a very large scale, it becomes absolutely necessary to reexamine the grounds on which these emendations are supposed to rest. There are, in fact, but few hymns in which some verses or some words have not been challenged for metrical reasons, and I feel bound, therefore, at the very beginning of my translation of the Rig-veda, to express my own opinion on this subject, and to give my reasons why in so many cases I allow metrical anomalies to remain which by some of the most learned and ingenious among Vedic scholars would be pronounced intolerable.

Even if the theory of the ancient metres had not been so carefully worked out by the authors of the Prâtisâkhyas and the Anukramanîs, an independent study of the Veda would have enabled us to discover the general rules by which the Vedic poets were guided in the composition of their works. Nor would it have been difficult to show how constantly these general principles are violated by the introduction of phonetic changes which in the later Sanskrit are called the euphonic changes of Sandhi, and according to which final vowels must be joined with initial vowels, and final consonants adapted to initial consonants, until at last each sentence becomes a continuous chain of closely linked syllables.

It is far easier, as I remarked before, to discover the original and natural rhythm of the Vedic hymns by reading them in the Pada than in the Samhitâ text, and after some practice our ear becomes sufficiently schooled to tell us at once how each line ought to be pronounced. We find, on the one hand, that the rules of Sandhi, instead of being generally binding, were treated by the Vedic poets as poetical licences only; and, on the other, that a greater freedom of pronunciation was allowed even in the body of words than would be tolerated in the later Sanskrit.

But what confirms me even more in my view that such strict uniformity must not be looked for in the ancient hymns of the Rishis, is the fact that in many cases it would he so very easy to replace the irregular by a regular dipodia. Supposing that the original poets had restricted themselves to the dijambus, who could have put in the place of that regular dijambus an irregular dipodia? Certainly not the authors of the Prâtisâkhya, for their ears had clearly discovered the general rhythm of the ancient metres; nor their predecessors, for they had in many instances preserved the tradition of syllables lengthened in accordance with the requirements of the metre. I do not mean to insist too strongly on this argument, or to represent those who handed down the tradition of the Veda as endowed with anything like apaurusheyatva. Strange accidents have happened in the text of the Veda, but they have generally happened when the sense of the hymns had ceased to be understood; and if anything helped to preserve the Veda from greater accidents, it was due, I believe, to the very fact that the metre continued to be understood, and that oral tradition, however much it might fail in other respects, had at all events to satisfy the ears of the hearers. I should have been much less surprised if all irregularities in the metre had been smoothed down by the flux and reflux of oral tradition, a fact which is so apparent in the text of Homer, where the gaps occasioned by the loss of the digamma, were made good by the insertion of unmeaning particles; but I find it difficult to imagine by what class of men, who must have lived between the original poets and the age of the Prâtisâkhyas, the simple rhythm of the Vedic metres should have been disregarded, and the sense of rhythm, which ancient people possess in a far higher degree than we ourselves, been violated through crude and purposeless alterations

...

Wherever we alter the text of the Rig-veda by conjecture, we ought to be able, if possible, to give some explanation how the mistake which we wish to remove came to be committed. If a passage is obscure, difficult to construe, if it contains words which occur in no other place, then we can understand how, during a long process of oral tradition, accidents may have happened. But when everything is smooth and easy, when the intention of the poet is not to be mistaken, when the same phrase has occurred many times before, then to suppose that a simple and perspicuous sentence was changed into a complicated and obscure string of words, is more difficult to understand.

The

Sacred Books of the East

Translated

By various Oriental scholars

and edited by

F. Max Müller

Vol. I

The Upanishads

Translated by F. Max Müller

In two parts

Part I

Oxford, the Clarendon Press

[1879]

TO

THE RIGHT HONOURABLE THE MARQUIS OF SALISBURY, K*G*.

CHANCELLOR OF THE UNIVERSITY OF OXFORD,

LATELY SECRETARY OF STATE FOR INDIA,

SIR HENRY J. S. MAINE, K.O*S*.I.

MEMBER OF THE COUNCIL OF INDIA,

AND

THE VERY REV. H. G. LIDDELL, D*D*.

DEAN OF CHRIST CHURCH,

TO WHOSE KIND INTEREST AND EXERTIONS

THIS ATTEMPT TO MAKE KNOWN TO THE ENGLISH PEOPLE

THE SACRED BOOKS OF THE EAST

IS SO LARGELY INDEBTED,

I NOW DEDICATE THESE VOLUMES WITH SINCERE RESPECT AND GRATITUDE,

F. MAX MÜLLER.

PREFACE

TO

THE SACRED BOOKS OF THE EAST

Most of the ancient sacred books have been handed down by oral tradition for many generations before they were consigned to writing....

Hence, what had been said by these half-human, half-divine ancestors, if it was preserved at all, was soon looked upon as a more than human utterance. It was received with reverence, it was never questioned and criticised.

Some of these ancient sayings were preserved because they were so true and so striking that they could not be forgotten. They contained eternal truths, expressed for the first time in human language.

Nor must we forget that though oral tradition, when once brought under proper discipline, is a most faithful guardian, it is not without its dangers in its incipient stages. Many a word may have been misunderstood, many a sentence confused, as it was told by father to son, before it became fixed in the tradition of a village community, and then resisted by its very sacredness all attempts at emendation.

Lastly, we must remember that those who handed down the ancestral treasures of ancient wisdom, would often feel inclined to add what seemed useful to themselves, and what they knew could be preserved in one way only, namely, if it was allowed to form part of the tradition that had to be handed down, as a sacred trust, from generation to generation. The priestly influence was at work, even before there were priests by profession, and when the priesthood had once become professional, its influence may account for much that would otherwise seem inexplicable in the sacred codes of the ancient world.

PROGRAM OF A TRANSLATION

OF

THE SACRED BOOKS OF THE EAST.

I here subjoin the program in which I first put forward the idea of a translation of the Sacred Books of the East, and through which I invited the co-operation of Oriental scholars in this undertaking. The difficulty of finding translators, both willing and competent to take a part in it, proved far greater than I had anticipated. Even when I had secured the assistance of a number of excellent scholars, and had received their promises of prompt co-operation, illness, domestic affliction, and even death asserted their control over all human affairs. Professor Childers, who had shown the warmest interest in our work, and on whom I chiefly depended for the Pali literature of the Buddhists, was taken from us, an irreparable loss to Oriental scholarship in general, and to our undertaking in particular. Among native scholars, whose co-operation I had been particularly desired to secure, Rajendralal Mitra, who had promised a translation of the Vâyu-purâ*na*, was prevented by serious illness from fulfilling his engagement. In other cases sorrow and sickness have caused, at all events, serious delay in the translation of the very books which were to have inaugurated this Series. However, new offers of assistance have come, and I hope that more may still come from Oriental scholars both in India and England, so that the limit of time which had been originally assigned to the publication of twenty-four volumes may not, I hope, be much exceeded.

THE SACRED BOOKS OF THE EAST, TRANSLATED, WITH INTRODUCTIONS AND NOTES, BY VARIOUS ORIENTAL SCHOLARS, AND EDITED BY F. MAX MULLER.

Apart from the interest which the Sacred Books of all religions possess in the eyes of the theologian, and, more particularly, of the missionary, to whom an accurate knowledge of them is as indispensable as a knowledge of the enemy's country is to a general, these works have of late assumed a new importance, as viewed in the character of ancient historical documents. In every country where Sacred Books have been preserved, whether by oral tradition or by writing, they are the oldest records, and mark the beginning of what may be called documentary, in opposition to purely traditional, history.

…

This being the case, it was but natural that the attention of the historian should of late have been more strongly attracted by these Sacred Books, as likely to afford most valuable information, not only on the religion, but also on the moral sentiments, the social institutions, the legal maxims of some of the most important nations of antiquity. There are not many nations that have preserved sacred writings, and many of those that have been preserved have but lately become accessible to us in their original form, through the rapid advance of Oriental scholarship in Europe. Neither Greeks, nor Romans, nor Germans, nor Celts, nor Slaves have left us anything that deserves the name of Sacred Books.

Oriental scholars have been blamed for not having as yet supplied a want so generally felt, and so frequently expressed, as a complete, trustworthy, and readable translation of the principal Sacred Books of the Eastern Religions. The reasons, however, why hitherto they have shrunk from such an undertaking are clear enough. The difficulties in many cases of giving complete translations, and not selections only, are very great. There is still much work to be done in a critical restoration of the original texts, in an examination of their grammar and metres, and in determining the exact meaning of many words and passages. That kind of work is naturally far more attractive to scholars than a mere translation, particularly when they cannot but feel that, with the progress of our knowledge, many a passage which now seems clear and easy, may, on being re-examined, assume a new import. Thus while scholars who are most competent to undertake a translation, prefer to devote their time to more special researches, the work of a complete translation is deferred to the future, and historians are left under the impression that Oriental scholarship is still in so unsatisfactory a state as to make any reliance on translations of the Veda, the Avesta, or the Tâo-te King extremely hazardous.

It is clear, therefore, that a translation of the principal Sacred Books of the East can be carried out only at a certain sacrifice. Scholars must leave for a time their own special researches in order to render the general results already obtained accessible to the public at large. And even then, really useful results can be achieved viribus unitis only. If four of the best Egyptologists have to combine in order to produce a satisfactory edition and translation of one of the Sacred Books of ancient Egypt, a much larger number of Oriental scholars will be required for translating the Sacred Books of the Brahmans, the Buddhists, the Zoroastrians, the followers of Khung-fû-ʒze, Lâo-ʒze, and Mohammed.

Lastly, there was the most serious difficulty of all, a difficulty which no scholar could remove, viz. the difficulty of finding the funds necessary for carrying out so large an undertaking. No doubt there exists at present a very keen interest in questions connected with the origin, the growth, and decay of religion. But much of that interest is theoretic rather than historical. How people might or could or should have elaborated religious ideas, is a topic most warmly discussed among psychologists and theologians, but a study of the documents, in which alone the actual growth of religious thought can be traced, is much neglected.

…

A faithful, unvarnished prose translation of the Sacred Books of India, Persia, China, and Arabia, though it may interest careful students, will never, I fear, excite a widespread interest, or command a circulation large enough to make it a matter of private enterprise and commercial speculation.

No doubt there is much in these old books that is startling by its very simplicity and truth, much that is elevated and elevating, much that is beautiful and sublime; but people who have vague ideas of primeval wisdom and the splendour of Eastern poetry will soon find themselves grievously disappointed. It cannot be too strongly stated, that the chief, and, in many cases, the only interest of the Sacred Books of the East is historical; that much in them is extremely childish, tedious, if not repulsive; and that no one but the historian will be able to understand the important lessons which they teach. It would have been impossible to undertake a translation even of the most important only of the Sacred Books of the East, without the support of an Academy or a University which recognises the necessity of rendering these works more generally accessible, on the same grounds on which it recognises the duty of collecting and exhibiting in Museums the petrifactions of bygone ages, little concerned whether the public admires the beauty of fossilised plants and broken skeletons, as long as hardworking students find there some light for reading once more the darker pages in the history of the earth.

Having been so fortunate as to secure that support, having also received promises of assistance from some of the best Oriental scholars in England and India, I hope I shall be able, after the necessary preparations are completed, to publish about three volumes of translations every year, selecting from the stores of the six so-called 'Book-religions' those works which at present can be translated, and which are most likely to prove useful. All translations will be made from the original texts, and where good translations exist already, they will be carefully revised by competent scholars. Such is the bulk of the religious literature of the Brahmans and the Buddhists, that to attempt a complete translation would be far beyond the powers of one generation of scholars. Still, if the interest in the work itself should continue, there is no reason why this series of translations should not be carried on, even after those who commenced it shall have ceased from their labours.

What I contemplate at present and I am afraid at my time of life even this may seem too sanguine, is no more than a Series of twenty-four volumes, the publication of which will probably extend over eight years.

POSITION OF THE UPANISHADS IN VEDIC LITERATURE.

My real love for Sanskrit literature was first kindled by the Upanishads. It was in the year 1844, when attending Schelling's lectures at Berlin, that my attention was drawn to those ancient theosophic treatises, and I still possess my collations of the Sanskrit MSS. which had then just arrived at Berlin, the Chambers collection, and my copies of commentaries, and commentaries on commentaries, which I made at that time. Some of my translations which I left with Schelling, I have never been able to recover, though to judge from others which I still possess, the loss of them is of small consequence. Soon after leaving Berlin, when continuing my Sanskrit studies at Paris under Burnouf, I put aside the Upanishads, convinced that for a true appreciation of them it was necessary to study, first of all, the earlier periods of Vedic literature, as represented by the hymns and the Brâhmanas of the Vedas.

In returning, after more than thirty years, to these favourite studies, I find that my interest in them, though it has changed in character, has by no means diminished.

It is true, no doubt, that the stratum of literature which contains the Upanishads is later than the Samhitâs, and later than the Brâhmanas, but the first germs of Upanishad doctrines go back at least as far as the Mantra period, which provisionally has been fixed between 1000 and 800 B.C. Conceptions corresponding to the general teaching of the Upanishads occur in certain hymns of the Rig-veda-samhitâ, they must have existed therefore before that collection was finally closed. One hymn in the Samhitâ of the Rig-veda (I, 191) was designated by Kâtyâyana, the author of the Sarvânukramanikâ, as an Upanishad. Here, however, upanishad means rather a secret charm than a philosophical doctrine. Verses of the hymns have often been incorporated in the Upanishads, and among the Oupnishads translated into Persian by Dârâ Shukoh we actually find the Purusha-sûkta, the 90th hymn of the tenth book of the Rig-veda, forming the greater portion of the Bark'heh Soukt. In the Samhitâ of the Yagur-veda, however, in the Vâgasaneyisâkhâ, we meet with a real Upanishad, the famous Îsâ or Îsâvâsya-upanishad, while the Sivasamkalpa, too, forms part of its thirty-fourth book. In the Brâhmanas several Upanishads occur, even in portions which are not classed as Âranyakas, as, for instance, the well-known Kena or Talavakâra upanishad. The recognised place, however, for the ancient Upanishads is in the Âranyakas, or forest-books, which, as a rule, form an appendix to the Brâhmanas, but are sometimes included also under the general name of Brâhmana. Brâhmana, in fact, meaning originally the sayings of Brahmans, whether in the general sense of priests, or in the more special of Brahman-priest, is a name applicable not only to the books, properly so called, but to all old prose traditions, whether contained in the Samhitâs, such as the Taittirîya-samhitâ, the Brâhmanas, the Âranyakas, the Upanishads, and even, in certain cases, in the Sûtras. We shall see in the introduction to the Aitareya-âranyaka, that that Âranyaka is in the beginning a Brâhmana, a mere continuation of the Aitareya-brâhmana, explaining the Mahâvrata ceremony, while its last book contains the Sûtras or short technical rules explaining the same ceremony which in the first book had been treated in the style peculiar to the Brâhmanas. In the same Aitareya-âranyaka, III, 2, 6, 6, a passage of the Upanishad is spoken of as a Brâhmana, possibly as something like a Brâhmana, while something very like an Upanishad occurs in the Âpastamba-sûtras, and might be quoted therefore as a Sûtra. At all events the Upanishads, like the Âranyakas, belong to what Hindu theologians call Sruti, or revealed literature, in opposition to Smriti, or traditional literature, which is supposed to be founded on the former, and allowed to claim a secondary authority only; and the earliest of these philosophical treatises will always, I believe, maintain a place in the literature of the world, among the most astounding productions of the human mind in any age and in any country.

DIFFERENT CLASSES OF UPANISHADS.

The ancient Upanishads, i. e. those which occupy a place in the Samhitâs, Brâhmanas, and Âranyakas, must be, if we follow the chronology which at present is commonly, though, it may be, provisionally only, received by Sanskrit scholars, older than 600 B.C., i.e. anterior to the rise of Buddhism. As to other Upanishads, and their number is very large, which either stand by themselves, or which are ascribed to the Atharva-veda, it is extremely difficult to fix their age. Some of them arc, no doubt, quite modern, for mention is made even of an Allah-upanishad; but others may claim a far higher antiquity than is generally assigned to them on internal evidence. I shall only mention that the name of Atharvasiras, an Upanishad generally assigned to a very modern date, is quoted in the Sûtras of Gautama and Baudhâyana; that the Svetâsvatara-upanishad, or the Svetâsvataranâm Mantropanishad, though bearing many notes of later periods of thought, is quoted by Saṅkara in his commentary on the Vedânta-sûtras; while the

Nrisimhottaratâpanîya-upanishad forms part of the twelve Upanishads explained by Vidyâranya in his Sarvopanishad-arthânubhûti-prakâsa. The Upanishads comprehended in that work are:

1. Aitareya-upanishad.

2. Taittirîya-upanishad.

3. Khândogya-upanishad.

4. Mundaka-upanishad.

5. Prasna-upanishad.

6. Kaushîtaki-upanishad.

7. Maitrâyanîya-upanishad.

8. Kathavallî-upanishad.

9. Svetâsvatara-upanishad.

10. Brihad-âranyaka-upanishad.

11. Talavakâra (Kena)-upanishad.

12. Nrisimhottaratâpanîya-upanishad 2.

The number of Upanishads translated by Dârâ Shukoh amounts to 50; their number, as given in the Mahâvâkyamuktâvalî and in the Muktikâ-upanishad, is 108. Professor Weber thinks that their number, so far as we know at present, may be reckoned at 235. In order, however, to arrive at so high a number, every title of an Upanishad would have to be counted separately, while in several cases it is clearly the same Upanishad which is quoted under different names. In an alphabetical list which I published in 1855 (Zeitschrift der Deutschen Morgenländischen Gesellschaft XIX, 137-158), the number of real Upanishads reached 149. To that number Dr. Burnell in his Catalogue (p. 59) added 5, Professor Haug (Brahma und die Brahmanen) 16, making a sum total of 170. New names, however, are constantly being added in the catalogues of MSS. published by Bühler, Kielhorn, Burnell, Rajendralal Mitra, and others, and I shall reserve therefore a more complete list of Upanishads for a later volume.

Though it is easy to see that these Upanishads belong to very different periods of Indian thought, any attempt to fix their relative age seems to me for the present almost hopeless. No one can doubt that the Upanishads which have had a place assigned to them in the Samhitâs, Brâhmanas, and Âranyakas are the oldest. Next to these we can draw a line to include the Upanishads clearly referred to in the Vedânta-sûtras, or explained and quoted by

Sankara, by Sâyana, and other more modern commentators. We can distinguish Upanishads in prose from Upanishads in mixed prose and verse, and again Upanishads in archaic verse from Upanishads in regular and continuous Anushtubh Slokas. We can also class them according to their subjects, and, at last, according to the sects to which they belong. But beyond this it is hardly safe to venture at present. Attempts have been made by Professor Weber and M. Regnaud to fix in each class the relative age of certain Upanishads, and I do not deny to their arguments, even where they conflict with each other, considerable weight in forming a preliminary judgment. But I know of hardly any argument which is really convincing, or which could not be met by counter arguments equally strong. Simplicity may be a sign of antiquity, but it is not so always, for what seems simple, may be the result of abbreviation. One Upanishad may give the correct, another an evidently corrupt reading, yet it does not follow that the correct reading may not be the result of an emendation. It is quite clear that a large mass of traditional Upanishads must have existed before they assumed their present form. Where two or three or four Upanishads contain the same story, told almost in the same words, they are not always copied from one another, but they have been settled independently, in different localities, by different teachers, it may be, for different purposes.

Lastly, the influence of Sâkhâs or schools may have told more or less on certain Upanishads. Thus the Maitrâyanîya-upanishad, as we now possess it, shows a number of irregular forms which even the commentator can account for only as peculiarities of the Maitrâyanîya-sâkhâ. That Upanishad, as it has come down to us, is full of what we should call clear indications of a modern and corrupt age. It contains in VI, 37, a sloka from the Mânava-dharma-sâstra, which startled even the commentator, but is explained away by him as possibly found in another Sâkhâ, and borrowed from there by Manu. It contains corruptions of easy words which one would have thought must have been familiar to every student. Thus instead of the passage as found in the Khândogya-upanishad VIII, 7, 1, ya âtmâpahatapâpmâ vigaro vimrityur visoko vigighatso pipâsah, &c., the text of the Maitrâyanîya-upanishad (VII, 7) reads, âtmâpahatapâpmâ vigaro vimrityur visoko vikikitso vipâsah. But here again the commentator explains that another Sâkhâ reads vigighatsa, and that avipâsa is to be explained by means of a change of letters as apipâsa. Corruptions, therefore, or modern elements which are found in one Upanishad, as handed down in one Sâkhâ, do not prove that the same existed in other Sâkhâs, or that they were found in the original text.

All these questions have to be taken into account before we can venture to give a final judgment on the relative age of Upanishads which belong to one and the same class. I know of no problem which offers so many similarities with the one before us as that of the relative age of the four Gospels. All the difficulties which occur in the Upanishads occur here, and no critical student who knows the difficulties that have to be encountered in determining the relative age of the four Gospels, will feel inclined, in the present state of Vedic scholarship, to speak with confidence on the relative age of the ancient Upanishads.

CRITICAL TREATMENT OF THE TEXT OF THE UPANISHADS.

With regard to a critical restoration of the text of the Upanishads, I have but seldom relied on the authority of new MSS., but have endeavoured throughout to follow that text which is presupposed by the commentaries, whether they are the work of the old Sankarâchârya, or of the more modern Sankarânanda, or Sâyana, or others. Though there still prevails some uncertainty as to the date of Sankarâchârya, commonly assigned to the eighth century A.D., yet I doubt whether any MSS. of the Upanishads could now be found prior to 1000 A.D. The text, therefore, which Sankara had before his eyes, or, it may be, his ears, commands, I think, a higher authority than that of any MSS. likely to be recovered at present.

It may be objected that *Sankara's* text belonged to one locality only, and that different readings and different recensions may have existed in other parts of India. That is perfectly true. We possess various recensions of several Upanishads, as handed down in different *Sâkhâs* of different Vedas, and we know of various readings recorded by the commentators. These, where they are of importance for our purposes, have been carefully taken into account.

It has also been supposed that *Sankara*, who, in writing his commentaries on the Upanishad, was chiefly guided by philosophical considerations, his chief object being to use the Upanishads as a sacred foundation for the Vedânta philosophy, may now and then have taken liberties with the text. That may be so, but no stringent proof of it has as yet been brought forward, and I therefore hold that when we succeed in establishing throughout that text which served as the basis of Sankara's commentaries, we have done enough for the present, and have fulfilled at all events the first and indispensable task in a critical treatment of the text of the Upanishads.

But in the same manner as it is easy to see that the text of the Rig-veda, which is presupposed by Sâyana's commentary and even by earlier works, is in many places palpably corrupt, we cannot resist the same conviction with regard to the text of the Upanishads. In some cases the metre, in others grammar, in others again the collation of analogous passages enable us to detect errors, and probably

very ancient errors, that had crept into the text long before
Śaṅkara composed his commentaries.

Some questions connected with the metres of the
Upanishads have been very learnedly treated by Professor
Gildemeister in his essay, 'Zur Theorie des Sloka.' The
lesson to be derived from that essay, and from a study of
the Upanishads, is certainly to abstain for the present from
conjectural emendations. In the old Upanishads the same
metrical freedom prevails as in the hymns; in the later
Upanishads, much may be tolerated as the result of
conscious or unconscious imitation. The metrical
emendations that suggest themselves are generally so easy
and so obvious that, for that very reason, we should
hesitate before correcting what native scholars would have
corrected long ago, if they had thought that there was any
real necessity for correction.

It is easy to suggest, for instance, that in the Vâgasaneyi-
samhitâ-upanishad, verse 5, instead of tad antar asya
sarvasya, tadu sarvasyâsya bâhyatah, the original text may
have been tad antar asya sarvasya tadu sarvasya bâhyatah;
yet Saṅkara evidently read sarvasyâsya, and as the same

71

reading is found in the text of the Vâgasaneyi-samhitâ, who would venture to correct so old a mistake?

Again, if in verse 8, we left out yâthâtathyatah, we should get a much more regular metre,

Kavir manîshî paribhûh svyambhûh
arthân vyadahâk khâsvatîbhyai samâbhyah.

Here vyada forms one syllable by what I have proposed to call synizesis, which is allowed in the Upanishads as well as in the hymns. All would then seem right, except that it is difficult to explain how so rare a word as yâthâtathyatah could have been introduced into the text.

In verse 10 one feels tempted to propose the omission of eva in anyad âhur avidyayâ, while in verse 11, an eva inserted after vidyâm ka would certainly improve the metre.

In verse 15 the expression satyadharmâya drishtaye is archaic, but perfectly legitimate in the sense of 'that we may see the nature of the True,' or 'that we see him whose nature is true.' When this verse is repeated in the Maitr. Up. VI, 35, we find instead, satyadharmâya vishnave, 'for the true Vishnu.' But here, again, no sound critic would venture to correct a mistake, intentional or unintentional, which is sanctioned both by the MSS. of the text and by the commentary.

Such instances, where every reader feels tempted at once to correct the textus receptus, occur again and again, and when they seem of any interest they have been mentioned in the notes. It may happen, however, that the correction, though at first sight plausible, has to be surrendered on more mature consideration. Thus in the Vâgasaneyi-samhitâ-upanishad, verse 2, one feels certainly inclined to write evam tve nânyatheto sti, instead of evam tvayi nânyatheto sti. But tve, if it were used here, would probably itself have to be pronounced dissyllabically, while tvayi, though it never occurs in the Rig-veda, may well keep its place here, in the last book of the Vâgasaneyi-samhitâ, provided we pronounce it by synizesis, i. e. as one syllable.

Attempts have been made sometimes to go beyond Sankara, and to restore the text, as it ought to have been originally, but as it was no longer in Sankara's time. It is one thing to decline to follow Sankara in every one of his interpretations, it is quite another to decline to accept the text which he interprets. The former is inevitable, the latter is always very precarious.

Thus I see, for instance, that M. Regnaud, in the Errata to the second volume of his excellent work on the Upanishads (Matériaux pour servir à l'histoire de la philosophie de l'Inde, 1878) proposes to read in the Brihad-âranyaka upanishad IV, 3, 1-8, sam anena vadishya iti, instead of sa mene na vadishya iti. Śankara adopted the latter reading, and explained accordingly, that Yâgñavalkya went to king Ganaka, but made up his mind not to speak. M. Regnaud, reading sam anena vadishya iti, takes the very opposite view, namely, that Yâgñavalkya went to king Ganaka, having made up his mind to have a conversation with him. As M. Regnaud does not rest this emendation on the authority of any new MSS., we may examine it as an ingenious conjecture; but in that case it seems to me clear that, if we adopted it, we should have at the same time to omit the whole sentence which follows. Śankara saw clearly that what had to be accounted or explained was why the king should address the Brahman first, samrâd eva pûrvam paprakkha; whereas if Yâgñavalkya had come with the intention of having a conversation with the king, he, the

Brahman, should have spoken first. This irregularity is explained by the intervening sentence, in which we are reminded that on a former occasion, when Ganaka and Yâgñavalkya had a disputation on the Agnihotra, Yâgñavalkya granted Ganaka a boon to choose, and he chose as his boon the right of asking questions according to his pleasure. Having received that boon, Ganaka was at liberty to question Yâgñavalkya, even though he did not like it, and hence Ganaka is introduced here as the first to ask a question.

All this hangs well together, while if we assume that Yâgñavalkya came for the purpose of having a conversation with Ganaka, the whole sentence from 'atha ha yag ganakas ka' to 'pûrvam paprakkha' would be useless, nor would there be any excuse for Ganaka beginning the conversation, when Yâgñavalkya came himself on purpose to question him.

It is necessary, even when we feel obliged to reject an interpretation of Saṅkara's, without at the same time altering the text, to remember that Saṅkara, where he is not blinded by philosophical predilections, commands the highest respect as an interpreter. I cannot help thinking therefore that M. Regnaud (vol. i, p. 59) was right in translating the passage in the Khând. Up. V, 3, 7, tasmâd u sarveshu lokeshu kshattrasyaiva praśâsanam abhût, by 'que le kshatriya seul l'a enseignée dans tous les mondes.' For when he proposes in the 'Errata' to translate instead, 'ç'est pourquoi l'empire dans tous les mondes fut attribué au kshatriya seulement,' he forgets that such an idea is foreign to the ordinary atmosphere in which the Upanishads move. It is not on account of the philosophical knowledge possessed by a few Kshatriyas, such as Ganaka or Pravâhana, that the privilege of government belongs everywhere to the second class. That rests on a totally different basis. Such exceptional knowledge, as is displayed by a few kings, might be an excuse for their claiming the privileges belonging to the Brahmans, but it would never, in the eyes of the ancient Indian Âryas, be considered as an argument for their claiming kingly power. Therefore, although I am well aware that prasâs is most frequently used in the sense of ruling, I have no doubt that Sankara likewise was fully aware of that, and that if he nevertheless explained prasâsana here in the sense of prasâstritvam sishyânâm, he did so because this meaning too was admissible, particularly here, where we may actually translate it by proclaiming, while the other meaning, that of ruling, would simply be impossible in the concatenation of ideas, which is placed before us in the Upanishad.

It seems, no doubt, extremely strange that neither the last redactors of the text of the Upanishads, nor the commentators, who probably knew the principal Upanishads by heart, should have perceived how certain passages in one Upanishad represented the same or nearly the same text which is found in another Upanishad, only occasionally with the most palpable corruptions.

Thus when the ceremony of offering a mantha or mash is described, we read in the Khândogya-upanishad V, 2, 6, that it is to be accompanied by certain words which on the whole are intelligible. But when the same passage occurs again in the Brihad-âranyaka, those words have been changed to such a degree, and in two different ways in the two Sâkhâs of the Mâdhyandinas and Kânvas, that, though the commentator explains them, they are almost unintelligible.

I shall place the three passages together in three parallel lines:

1. Khândogya-upanishad V, 2, 6:
II. Brihad-âranyaka, Mâdhyandina-sâkhâ, XIV, 9, 3, 10:
III. Brihad-âranyaka-upanishad, Kânva-sâkhâ, VI, 3, 5:

I. Amo nâmâsy amâ hi te sarvam idam sa hi gyeshthah
II. âmo 'sy âmam hi te mayi sa hi
III. âmamsy âmamhi te mahi sa hi

I. sreshtho râgâdhipatih sa mâ gyaishthyam srai-
II. râgesâno 'dhipatih sa mâ râgesâno
III. râgesâno

I. shthyam râgyam âdhipatyam gamayatv aham evedam
II. 'dhipatim karotv iti.
III. 'dhipatim karotv iti.

I. sarvam asânîti.
II.
III.

The text in the Khândogya-upanishad yields a certain sense, viz. 'Thou art Ama by name, for all this together exists in thee. He is the oldest and best, the king, the sovereign. May he make me the oldest, the best, the king, the sovereign. May I be all this.' This, according to the commentator, is addressed to Prâna, and Ama, though a purely artificial word, is used in the sense of Prâna, or breath, in another passage also, viz. Brihad-âranyaka-up. I, 3, 22. If therefore we accept this meaning of Ama, the rest is easy and intelligible.

But if we proceed to the Brihad-âranyaka, in the Mâdhyandina-sâkhâ, we find the commentator proposing the following interpretation: 'O Mantha, thou art a full knower, complete knowledge of me belongs to thee.' This meaning is obtained by deriving âmah from â + man, in the sense of knower, and then taking âmam, as a neuter, in the sense of knowledge, derivations which are simply impossible.

Lastly, if we come to the text of the Kânva-sâkhâ, the grammatical interpretation becomes bolder still. Sankara does not explain the passage at all, which is strange, but Ânandagiri interprets âmamsi tvam by 'Thou knowest (all),' and âmamhi te mahi, by 'we know thy great (shape),' which are again impossible forms.

But although there can be little doubt here that the reading of the Khândogya-upanishad gives us the original text, or a text nearest to the original, no sound critic would venture to correct the readings of the Brihad-âranyaka. They are corruptions, but even as corruptions they possess authority, at all events up to a certain point, and it is the fixing of those certain points or chronological limits, which alone can impart a scientific character to our criticism of ancient texts.

In the Kaushîtaki-brâhmana-upanishad Professor Cowell has pointed out a passage to me, where we must go beyond the text as it stood when commented on by the Sankarânanda. In the beginning of the fourth adhyâya all MSS. of the text read savasan, and this is the reading which the commentator seems anxious to explain, though not very successfully. I thought that possibly the commentator might have had before him the reading sa vasan, or so 'vasan, but both would be very unusual. Professor Cowell in his Various Readings, p. xii, conjectured samvasan, which would be liable to the same objection. He now, however, informs me that, as B. has samtvan, and C. satvan, he believes the original text to have been Satvan-Matsyeshu. This seems to me quite convincing, and is borne out by the reading of the Berlin MS., so far as it can be made out from Professor Weber's essay on the Upanishads, Indische Studien I, p.419. I see that Boehtlingk and Roth in their Sanskrit Dictionary, sv. satvat, suggest the same emendation.

The more we study the nature of Sanskrit MSS., the more, I believe, we shall feel convinced that their proper arrangement is one by locality rather than by time. I have frequently dwelt on this subject in the introductions to the successive volumes of my edition of the Rig-veda and its commentary by Sâyanâkârya, and my convictions on this point have become stronger ever since. A MS., however modern, from the south of India or from the north, is more important as a check on the textus receptus of any Sanskrit work, as prevalent in Bengal or Bombay, than ever so many MSS., even if of greater antiquity, from the same locality. When therefore I was informed by my friend Dr. Bühler that he had discovered in Kashmir a MS. of the

Aitareya-upanishad, I certainly expected some real help from such a treasure. The MS. is described by its discoverer in the last number of the journal of the Bombay Asiatic Society, p. 34, and has since been sent to me by the Indian Government. It is written on birch bark (bhûrga), and in the alphabet commonly called Sâradâ. The leaves are very much injured on the margin and it is almost impossible to handle them without some injury. In many places the bark has shrunk, probably on being moistened, and the letters have become illegible. Apart from these drawbacks, there remain the difficulties inherent in the Sâradâ alphabet which, owing to its numerous combinations, is extremely difficult to read, and very trying to eyes which are growing weak. However, I collated the Upanishad from the Aitareya-âranyaka, which turned out to be the last portion only, viz. the Samhitâ-upanishad (Ait. Âr. III, 1-2), or, as it is called here, Samhitâranya, and I am sorry to say my expectations have been disappointed. The MS. shows certain graphic peculiarities which Dr. Bühler has pointed out. It is particularly careful in the use of the sibilants, replacing the Visarga by sibilants, writing s + s and s + s instead of h + s and h + s; distinguishing also the Gihvâmûlîya and Upadhmanîya. If therefore the MS. writes

82

antastha, we may be sure that it really meant to write so, and not antahstha, or, as it would have written, antasstha. It shows equal care in the use of the nasals, and generally carries on the sandhi between different paragraphs. Here and there I met with better readings than those given in Rajendralal Mitra's edition, but in most cases the commentary would have been sufficient to restore the right reading. A few various readings, which seemed to deserve being mentioned, will be found in the notes. The MS., though carefully written, is not free from the ordinary blunders. At first one feels inclined to attribute some importance to every peculiarity of a new MS., but very soon one finds out that what seems peculiar, is in reality carelessness. Thus Ait. Âr. III, I, 5, 2, the Kashmir MS. has pûrvam aksharam rûpam, instead of what alone can be right, pûrvarûpam. Instead of pragayâ pasubhih it writes repeatedly pragaya pasubhih, which is impossible. In III, 2, 2, it leaves out again and again manomaya between khandomaya and vânmaya; but that this is a mere accident we learn later on, where in the same sentence manomayo, is found in its right place. Such cases reduce this MS. to its proper level, and make us look with suspicion on any accidental variations, such as I have noticed in my translation.

The additional paragraph, noticed by Dr. Bühler, is very indistinct, and contains, so far as I am able to find out, sânti verses only.

I have no doubt that the discovery of new MSS. of the Upanishads and their commentaries will throw new light on the very numerous difficulties with which a translator of the Upanishads, particularly in attempting a complete and faithful translation, has at present to grapple. Some of the difficulties, which existed thirty years ago, have been removed since by the general progress of Vedic scholarship, and by the editions of texts and commentaries and translations of Upanishads, many of which were known at that time in manuscript only. But I fully agree with M. Regnaud as to the difficultés considérables que les meilleures traductions laissent subsister, and which can be solved only by a continued study of the Upanishads, the Âranyakas, the Brâhmanas, and the Vedânta-sûtras.

I.

THE KHÂNDOGYA-UPANISHAD.

THE Khândogya-upanishad belongs to the Sâma-veda.
Together with the Brihad-âranyaka, which belongs to the
Yagur-veda, it has contributed the most important
materials to what may be called the orthodox philosophy of
India, the Vedânta, i.e. the end, the purpose, the highest
object of the Veda. It consists of eight adhyâyas or lectures,
and formed part of a Khândogya-brâhmana, in which it
was preceded by two other adhyâyas. While MSS. of the
Khândogya-upanishad and its commentary are frequent, no
MSS. of the whole Brâhmana has been met with in Europe.
Several scholars had actually doubted its existence, but
Rajendralal Mitra, in the Introduction to his translation of
the Khândogya-upanishad, states that in India 'MSS. of the
work are easily available, though as yet he has seen no
commentary attached to the Brâhmana portion of any one
of them.' 'According to general acceptation,' he adds, 'the
work embraces ten chapters, of which the first two are
reckoned to be the Brâhmana, and the rest is known under
the name of Khândogya-upanishad. In their arrangement

and style the two portions differ greatly, and judged by them they appear to be productions of very different ages, though both are evidently relics of pretty remote antiquity. Of the two chapters of the Khândogya-brâhmana, the first includes eight sûktas (hymns) on the ceremony of marriage, and the rites necessary to be observed at the birth of a child. The first sûktas is intended to be recited when offering an oblation to Agni on the occasion of a marriage, and its object is to pray for prosperity in behalf of the married couple. The second prays for long life, kind relatives, and a numerous progeny. The third is the marriage pledge by which the contracting parties bind themselves to each other. Its spirit may be guessed from a single verse. In talking of the unanimity with which they will dwell, the bridegroom addresses his bride, "That heart of thine shall be mine, and this heart of mine shall be thine." The fourth and the fifth invoke Agni, Vâyu, Kandramas, and Sûrya to bless the couple and ensure healthful progeny. The sixth is a mantra for offering an oblation on the birth of a child; and the seventh and the eighth are prayers for its being healthy, wealthy, and powerful, not weak, poor, or mute, and to ensure a profusion of wealth and milch-cows. The first sûkta of the second chapter is addressed to the Earth, Agni, and Indra, with a prayer for wealth, health, and prosperity; the second, third, fourth, fifth, and sixth are mantras for offering oblations to cattle, the manes, Sûrya, and divers minor deities. The seventh is a curse upon worms, insects, flies, and other nuisances, and the last, the concluding mantra of the marriage ceremony, in which a general blessing is invoked for all concerned.'

After this statement there can be but little doubt that this Upanishad originally formed part of a Brâhmana. This may have been called either by a general name, the Brâhmana of the Khandogas, the followers of the Sâma-veda, or, on account of the prominent place occupied in it by the Upanishad, the Upanishad-brâhmana. In that case it would be one of the eight Brâhmanas of the Sâma-veda, enumerated by Kumârila Bhatta and others, and called simply Upanishad, scil. Brâhmana.

The text of the Upanishad with the commentary of Śankara and the gloss of Ânandagiri has been published in the Bibliotheca Indica. The edition can only claim the character of a manuscript, and of a manuscript not always very correctly read.

A translation of the Upanishad was published, likewise in the Bibliotheca Indica, by Rajendralal Mitra.

It is one of the Upanishads that was translated into Persian under the auspices of Dârâ Shukoh, and from Persian into French by Anquetil Duperron, in his Oupnekhat, i.e. *Secretum Tegendum*. Portions of it were translated into English by Colebrooke in his Miscellaneous Essays, into Latin and German by F. W. Windischmann, in his Sankara, seu de theologumenis Vedanticorum. (Bonn, 1833), and in a work published by his father, K. J. H. Windischmann, Die Philosophie im Fortgang der Weltgeschichte (Bonn, 1827-34). Professor A. Weber has treated of this Upanishad in his Indische Studien I, 254; likewise M. P. Regnaud in his Matériaux pour servir à l'histoire dc la philosophie de l'Inde (Paris, 1876) and Mr. Gough in several articles on 'the Philosophy of the Upanishads,' in the Calcutta Review, No. CXXXI.

I have consulted my predecessors whenever there was a serious difficulty to solve in the translation of these ancient texts. These difficulties are very numerous, as those know best who have attempted to give complete translations of these ancient texts. It will be seen that my translation differs sometimes very considerably from those of my predecessors. Though I have but seldom entered into any controversy with them, they may rest assured that I have not deviated from them without careful reflection.

LECTURE III.

THE ANCIENT LITERATURE OF INDIA

SO FAR AS IT SUPPLIES MATERIALS

FOR THE STUDY OF THE ORIGIN

OF RELIGION[8]

---

[8] *Lectures on the Origin and Growth of Religion. As Illustrated by the Religions of India.* Max Mueller (New York: Charles Scribner's Sons, 1879). pp. 124-153.

...

Discovery of Sanskrit literature.

The discovery of the ancient literature of India must sound
to most people like a fairy-tale rather than like a chapter of
history, nor do I wonder that there is, or that there has
been at least for a long time, a certain incredulity, with
regard to the genuineness of that literature. The number of
separate works in Sanskrit, of which manuscripts are still in
existence, is now estimated to amount to about 10,000.[9]
What would Plato and Aristotle have said, if they had been
told that at their time there existed in India, in that India
which Alexander had just discovered, if not conquered, an

---

[9] Rajendralal Mitra, ' Catalogue of Sanskrit MSS. in the Library of the
Asiatic Library of Bengal,' 1877, Preface, p. 1. The India Office
Library is said to contain 4093 separate codices; the Bodleian 854, the
Berlin library about the same number. The library of the Maharaja of
Tanjore is estimated at upwards of 18000, in eleven distinct
alphabets; the library of the Sanskrit College at Benares at 2000; the
library of the Asiatic Society of Bengal at Calcutta at 37003 that of
the Sanskrit College at Calcutta at 2000.

ancient literature far richer than anything they possessed at that time in Greece?

The Veda handed down by oral tradition.

But how, you may ask, was that ancient literature preserved? At present, no doubt, there are MSS. of the Veda, but few Sanskrit MSS. in India are older than 1000 after Christ, nor is there any evidence that the art of writing was known in India much before the beginning of Buddhism, or the very end of the ancient Vedic literature. How then were these ancient hymns, and the Brahmanas, and it may be, the Sutras too, preserved? Entirely by memory, but by memory kept under the strictest discipline. As far back as we know anything of India, we find that the years which we spend at school and at university, were spent by the sons of the three higher classes, in learning from the mouth of a teacher, their sacred literature. This was a sacred duty, the neglect of which entailed social degradation, and the most minute rules were laid down as to the mnemonic system that had to be followed. Before the invention of writing, there was no other way of preserving literature, whether sacred or profane, and in consequence every precaution was taken against accidents.

It has sometimes been asserted that the Vedic religion is extinct in India, that it never recovered from its defeat by Buddhism; that the modern Brahmanic religion, as founded on the Puranas and Tantras, consists in a belief in Vishnu, Siva, and Brahma, and manifests itself in the worship of the most hideous idols. To a superficial observer it may seem to be so, but English scholars who have lived in India in intimate relations with the natives, or native scholars who now occasionally visit us in England, give a very different account. No doubt, Brahmanism was for a time defeated by Buddhism; no doubt it had, at a later time, to accommodate itself to circumstances, and tolerate many of the local forms of worship, which were established in India, before it was slowly subdued by the Brahmans. Nor did Brahmanism ever possess a state machinery to establish uniformity of religious belief, to test orthodoxy, or to punish heresy over the whole of India. But how was it that, during the late famine, many people would rather die than accept food from unclean hands? Are there any priests in

Europe or elsewhere, whose authority would be proof against starvation? The influence of the priests is still enormous in India, and all the greater, because it is embodied in the influence of custom, tradition, and superstition. Now those men who are, even at the present moment, recognised as the spiritual guides of the people, those whose influence for good or evil is even now immense, are believers in the supreme authority of the Veda. Everything, whether founded on individual opinion, on local custom, on Tantras or Puranas, nay, even on the law-books of Manu, must give way, as soon as it can be proved to be in direct conflict with a single sentence of the Veda. On that point there can be no controversy. But those Brahmans, who even in this Kali age, and during the ascendency of the Mlechas, uphold the sacred traditions of the past, are not to be met with in the drawing-rooms of Calcutta. They depend on the alms of the people, and live in villages, either by themselves, or in colleges. They would lose their prestige, if they were to shake hands or converse with an infidel, and it is only in rare cases that they drop their reserve, when brought in contact with Europeans whose knowledge of their own sacred language and literature excites their wonderment, and with a little pressure, opens their heart and their mouth, like a treasure-house of ancient knowledge. Of course, they would not speak English or even Bengali. They speak Sanskrit and write Sanskrit, and I frequently receive letters from some of them, couched in the most faultless language.

And my fairy-tale is not all over yet. These men, and I know it as a fact, know the whole Rig-Veda by heart, just as their ancestors did, three or four thousand years ago; and though they have MSS., and though they now have a printed text, they do not learn their sacred lore from them. They learn it, as their ancestors learnt it, thousands of years ago, from the mouth of a teacher, so that the Vedic succession should never be broken.[10] That oral teaching

---

[10] This oral teaching is carefully described in the Pratisakhya of the Rig-Veda, i. e., probably in the fifth or sixth century B. C. It is constantly alluded to in the Brahmanas, but it must have existed even during the earlier periods, for in a hymn of the Rig-Veda (VII. 103), in which the return of the rainy season, and the delight and quacking of the frogs is described, we read: "One repeats the speech of the other, as the pupil (repeats the words) of the teacher." The pupil is called sikshamanah, the teacher saktah, while siksha, from the same root, is the recognized technical term for phonetics in later times.

and learning became in the eyes of the Brahmans one of the great sacrifices, and though the number of those who still keep it up is smaller than it used to be, their influence, their position, their sacred authority, are as great as ever. These men do not come to England, they would not cross the sea. But some of their pupils, who have been brought up half on the native, and half on the English system, are less strict. I have had visits from natives who knew large portions of the Veda by heart; I have been in correspondence with others who, when they were twelve or fifteen years old, could repeat the whole of it.[11] They learn a few lines every day, repeat them for hours, so that the whole house resounds with the noise, and they thus strengthen their memory to that degree, that when their apprenticeship is finished, you can open them like a book, and find any passage you like, any word, any accent. One native scholar, Shankar Pandurang, is at the present moment collecting various readings for my edition of the Rig-Veda, not from MSS., but from the oral tradition of Vaidik Srotriyas. He writes, on the 2nd March, 1877,

---

[11] *Indian Antiquary,* 1878, p. 140. "There are thousands of Brahmans, the editor remarks, who know the whole of the Rig-Veda by heart, and can repeat it, etc."

I am collecting a few of our walking Rig-Veda MSS., taking your text as the basis. I find a good many differences which I shall soon be able to examine more closely, when I may be able to say whether they are various readings, or not. I will, of course, communicate them all to you before making any use of them publicly, if I ever do this at all. As I write, a Vaidik scholar is going over your Rig-Veda text. He has his own MS. on one side, but does not open it, except occasionally. He knows the whole Samhita and Pada texts by heart. I wish I could send you his photograph, how he is squatting in my tent with his Upavita (the sacred cord) round his shoulders, and only a Doti round his middle, not a bad specimen of our old Bishis.'

Think of that half-naked Hindu, repeating under an Indian sky the sacred hymns which have been handed down for three or four thousand years by oral tradition. If writing had never been invented, if printing had never been invented, if India had never been occupied by England, that young Brahman, and hundreds and thousands of his countrymen would probably have been engaged just the same in learning and saying by heart the simple prayers first uttered on the Sarasvati, and the other rivers of the Punjab by Vasishita, Visvamitra, Syavasva, and others. And here are we, under the shadow of Westminster Abbey, in the very zenith of the intellectual life of Europe, nay, of the whole world, listening in our minds to the same sacred hymns, trying to understand them (and they are sometimes very difficult to understand), and hoping to learn from them some of the deepest secrets of the human heart, that human heart which is the same everywhere, however widely we ourselves may be separated from each other by space and time, by colour and creed.

This is the story I wished to tell you to-day. And though it may have sounded to some of you like a fairy-tale, believe me it is truer in all its details than many a chapter of contemporary history.

POSTSCRIPT TO THE THIRD LECTURE.

As I find that some of my remarks as to the handing down of the ancient Sanskrit literature by means of oral tradition, and the permanence of that system to the present day have been received with a certain amount of incredulity, I subjoin some extracts from the Rig-veda-pratisakhya, to show how the oral teaching of the Vedas was carried on at least 500 B.C., and some statements from the pen of two native scholars, to show how it is maintained to the present day.

The Pratisakhya of the Rig-Veda, of which I published the text and a German translation in 1856, contains the rules according to which the sacred texts are to be pronounced. I still ascribe this, which seems to me the oldest Pratisakhya, to the 5th or 6th century B.C, to a period between Yaska on one side, and Panini on the other, until more powerful arguments can be brought forward against this date than have been hitherto advanced. In the 15th chapter of that Pratisakhya we find a description of the method followed in the schools of ancient India. The teacher, we are told, must himself have passed through the recognised curriculum, and have fulfilled all the duties of a Brahmanical student (brahmakarin), before he is allowed to become a teacher, and he must teach such students only who submit to all the rules of studentship. He should settle down in a proper place. If he has only one pupil or two, they should sit on his right side; if more, they must sit as there is room for them. At the beginning of each lecture the pupils embrace the feet of their teacher, and say: Read, Sir. The teacher answers: Om, Yes, and then pronounces two words, or, if it is a compound, one. When the teacher has pronounced one word or two, the first pupil repeats the first word, but if there is anything that requires explanation, the pupil says Sir; and after it has been explained to him (the teacher says), Om, Yes, Sir.

In this manner they go on till they have finished a prasna (question), which consists of three verses, or, if they are verses of more than forty to forty two syllables, of two verses. If they are pankti verses of forty to forty-two syllables each, a prasna may comprise either two or three; and if a hymn consists of one verse only, that is supposed to form a prasna. After the prasna is finished, they have all to repeat it once more, and then to go on learning it by heart, pronouncing every syllable with the high accent. After the teacher has first told a prasna to his pupil on the right, the others go round him to the right, and this goes on till the whole adhyaya or lecture is finished; a lecture consisting generally of sixty prasnas. At the end of the last half-verse the teacher says Sir, and the pupil replies, Om, Yes, Sir, repeating also the verses required at the end of a lecture. The pupils then embrace the feet of their teacher, and are dismissed.

These are the general features of a lesson, but the Pratisakhya contains a number of minute rules besides. For instance, in order to prevent small words from being neglected, the teacher is to repeat twice every word which has but one high accent, or consists of one vowel only. A number of small words are to be followed by the particle *iti*, thus; others are to be followed by *iti*, and then to be repeated again, e.g. ka-iti *ka*.

These lectures continued during about half the year, the term beginning generally with the rainy season. There were, however, many holidays on which no lectures were given, and on these points also the most minute regulations are given both in the Grihya and Dharma-sutras.

This must suffice as a picture of what took place in India about 500 B.C. Let us now see what remains of the ancient system at present.

In a letter received from the learned editor of the "Shaddarsana-kintanika," or *Studies in Indian Philosophy*, dated Poona, 8 June, 1878, the writer says:

A student of a Rig-Veda-sakha (a recension of the Rig-Veda), if sharp and assiduous, takes about eight years to learn the Dasagranthas, the ten books, which consist of

(1) The Samhita, or the hymns.

(2) The Brahmana, the prose treatise on sacrifices, etc.

(3) The Aranyaka, the forest-book.

(4) The Grihya-sutras, the rules on domestic ceremonies.

(5-10) The six Angas, treatises on Siksha, pronunciation, Gyotisha, astronomy, Kalpa, ceremonial, Vyakarana, grammar, Nighantu and Nirukta, etymology, khanddas, metre

A pupil studies every day during the eight years, except on the holidays, the so-called anadhyaya, i. e. non-reading days. There being 360 days in a lunar year, the eight years would give him 2880 days. From this 384 holidays have to be deducted, leaving him 2496 work-days during the eight years.

Now the ten books consist on a rough calculation of 29,500 slokas, so that a student of the RigVeda has to learn about twelve slokas a day, a sloka consisting of thirty-two syllables.

I ought to point out to you the source of my information. We have an association in Poona which is called the Vedasastrottegakasabha, which annually awards prizes in all recognised branches of Sanskrit learning, such as the six schools of Indian philosophy, the Alankara-sastra or rhetoric, Vaidyaka or medicine, Gyotisha or astronomy, recitation of the Veda in its different forms, such as Pada,

Krama, Ghana, and *Gata,* and all the subjects I have already mentioned under the name of Dasagrantha, in the case of the Rig-veda Brahmans. The prize-men are recommended by a board of examiners. In every subject a threefold test is employed,—theoretical knowledge of the subject (prakriya), general knowledge of the subject (upasthiti), and the construction of passages from recognised works in each branch of knowledge (grantharthapariksha). About 1000 rupees are distributed by the leading native gentlemen of Poona. At a meeting held the 8th May last there were about fifty Sanskrit Pandits and Vaidikas. In their presence I got the information from an old Vaidika much respected in Poona.

Another interesting account of the state of native learning comes from the pen of Professor E. G-. Bhandarkar, M. A. ('Indian Antiquary,' 1874, p. 132):

'Every Brahmanic family,' he writes, 'is devoted to the study of a particular Veda, and a particular sakha (recension) of a Veda; and the domestic rites of the family are performed according to the ritual described in the Sutra connected with that Veda

The study consists in getting by heart the books forming the particular Veda. In Northern India, where the predominant Veda is the White Yagush, and the sakha that of the Madhyandinas, this study has almost died out, except at Banaras, where Brahmanic families from all parts of India are settled. It prevails to some extent in Gujarat, but to a much greater extent in the Maratha country; and in Tailangana there is a large number of Brahmans who still devote their life to this study. Numbers of these go about to all parts of the country in search of dakshina (fee, alms), and all well-to-do natives patronize them according to their means, by getting them to repeat portions of their Veda, which is mostly the Black Yagush, with Apastamba for their Sutra. Hardly a week passes here in Bombay in which no Tailangana Brahman comes to me to ask for dakshina. On each occasion I get the men to repeat what they have learned, and compare it with the printed texts in my possession.

With reference to their occupation, Brahmans of each Veda are generally divided into two classes, Grihasthas and Bhikshukas. The former devote themselves to a worldly avocation, while the latter spend their time in the study of their sacred books and the practice of their religious rites.

Both these classes have to repeat daily the Sandhya-vandana or twilight-prayers, the forms of which are somewhat different for the different Vedas. But the repetition of the Gayatri-mantra 'Tat Savitur varenyam,' etc., five, ten, twenty-eight, or a hundred and eight times, which forms the principal portion of the ceremony, is common to all.

. . . .

These extracts will show what can be done by memory for the preservation of an ancient literature. The texts of the

Veda have been handed down to us with such accuracy that there is hardly a various reading in the proper sense of the word, or even an uncertain accent, in the whole of the Rig-Veda. There are corruptions in the text, which can be discovered by critical investigation; but even these corruptions must have formed part of the recognised text since it was finally settled. Some of them belong to different /Sakhas or recensions, and are discussed in their bearing by ancient authorities.

The authority of the Veda, in respect to all religious questions, is as great in India now as it has ever been. It never was uncontested as little as the authority of any other sacred book has been. But to the vast majorities of orthodox believers the Veda forms still the highest and only infallible authority, quite as much as the Bible with us, or the Koran with the Mohammedans.

OTHER SOURCES.

The translator of the following text – draws attention to the hymns that comprise the SamaVeda – namely – that they were taken from the RigVeda and rearranged; thus – we can conclude that the authors of the SamaVeda – themselves participated in acts of collation and transference from an existing text. It draws attention to the role of authorial intention in the Vedic period.

The Collection is made up of hymns, portions of hymns, and detached verses, taken mainly from the *Rgveda*, transposed and re-arranged, without reference to their original order, to suit the religious ceremonies in which they were to be employed.

HYMNS OF THE SAMAVEDA[12]

Translated with a Popular Commentary

Ralph T.H. Griffith

1895

PREFACE

The Collection is made up of hymns, portions
of hymns, and detached verses, taken mainly
from the *Rgveda*, transposed and re-arranged,
without reference to their original order, to suit
the religious ceremonies in which they were to
be employed. In these compiled hymns there
are frequent variations, of more or less
importance, from the text of the *Rgveda* as we
now possess it which variations, although in
some cases they are apparently explanatory,

---

[12] *Internet Sacred Texts Archives*, edited by John B. Hare, 2008, www.sacred-texts.com.

seem in others to be older and more original than the readings of the *Rgveda.* In singing, the verses are still further altered by prolongation, repetition and insertion of syllables, and various modulations, rests, and other modifications prescribed, for the guidance of the officiating priests, in the Ganas or Song-books. Two of these manuals, the Gramageyagdna, or Congregational, and the Aranyagana or Forest Song-Book, follow the order of the verses of part I, of the Sanhita, and two others, the Uhagana, the Uhyagana, of Part II. This part is less disjointed than part I, and is generally arranged in triplets whose first verse is often the repetition of a verse that has occurred in part I.

...

There are three recensions of the text of the *Samaveda Sanhita,* the Kauthuma Sakha or recension is current in Guzerat, the Jaiminiya in the Carnatic, and the Ranayaniya in the Mahratta country. A translation, by Dr. Stevenson, of the Ranayaniya recension-or, rather, a free version of Sayana's paraphrase-was edited by Professor Wilson, in 1842; in 1848 Professor Benfey of Göttingen brought out an excellent edition of the same text with a metrical translation, a complete glossary, and explanatory notes; and in 1874-78 Pandit Satyavrata Samasrami of Calcutta published in the Bibliotheca Indicaa. most meritorious edition of the Sanhita according to the same recension, with Sayana's commentary, portions of the Song-books, and other illustrative matter. I have followed Benfey's text, and have, made much use of his glossary and notes. Pandit Satyavrata Samasrami's edition also has been of the greatest service to me. To Mr. Venis, Principal of the Benares Sanskrit College, I am indebted for, the loan of the College manuscripts of the text and commentary.

NOTES:

ABOUT OPEN WINDOWS: A FEMINIST RESOURCE
CENTER

ABOUT THE AUTHOR

O₂pen Windows: A Feminist Resource and Research Center.

O₂pen Windows is a feminist research cum *adda* center, based in Bangalore. If it could, it would sustain itself with endless cups of tea and lots of stimulating research.

The Purpose: O₂pen Windows encourages research on both contemporary and historical socio-cultural issues and literary issues. These findings will subsequently be documented, archived and published as monographs and essays.

For more information, write to: openwindows101@gmail.com.

VISIT US AT: www.aresourcecenter.wordpress.com.